A BRIEF DESCRIPTION
OF THE COCKATIEL

A GUIDE ON BREEDING, HABITAT,
HABITS AND HOW TO TRAIN, TAME
AND CARE FOR YOUR COCKATIEL

British Library Cataloguing-in-Publication Data
A catalogue record for this book is available from the
British Library

CONTENTS

AVICULTURE 1

THE BREEDING OF COCKATIELS 7

THE COCKATIEL - HABITAT AND WILD
LIFE 10

THE COCKATIEL - HOW TO BREED, TAME,
AND TEACH TO TALK 17

Aviculture

'Aviculture' is the practice of keeping and breeding birds, as well as the culture that forms around it, and there are various reasons why people get involved in Aviculture. Some people breed birds to preserve a specific species, usually due to habitat destruction, and some people breed birds (especially parrots) as companions, and yet others do this to make a profit. Aviculture encourages conservation, provides education about avian species, provides companion birds for the public, and includes research on avian behaviour. It is thus a highly important and enjoyable past time. There are avicultural societies throughout the world, but generally in Europe, Australia and the United States, where people tend to be more prosperous, having more leisure time to invest. The first avicultural society in Australia was The Avicultural Society of South Australia, founded in 1928. It is now promoted with the name Bird Keeping in Australia. The two major national avicultural societies in the United States are the American Federation of Aviculture and the Avicultural Society of America, founded in 1927. In the UK, the Avicultural Society was formed in 1894 and the Foreign Bird League in 1932. The Budgerigar Society was formed in 1925.

Some of the most popular domestically kept birds are finches and canaries. 'Finches' are actually a broader category, encompassing canaries, and make fantastic domestic birds, capable of living long and healthy lives if given the requisite care. Most species are very easy to breed, and usefully do not grow too large (unlike their larger compatriot the budgerigar), and so do not need a massive living space. 'Canary' (associated with the Serinus canaria), is a song bird is native to the Canary Islands, Madeira, and the Azores – and has long been kept as a cage bird in Europe, beginning in the 1470s. It now enjoys an international following, and the terms canariculture and canaricultura have been used in French, Spanish and Italian respectively, to describe the keeping and breeding of canaries. It is only gradually however (a testament to its growing popularity) that English breeders are beginning to use such terms. Canaries are now the most popular form of finch kept in Britain and are often found still fulfilling their historic role of protecting underground miners. Canaries like budgies, are seed eaters, which need to dehusk the seed before feeding on the kernel. However, unlike budgerigars, canaries are perchers. The average life span of a canary is five years, although they have been known to live twice as long.

Parakeets or 'Budgies' (a type of parrot) are another incredibly popular breed of domestic bird, and are originally from Australia, first brought to Europe in the 1840s. Whilst they are naturally green with yellow heads and black bars on the wings in the wild, domesticated budgies come in a massive variety of colours. They have the toes and beak typical of parrot like birds, as in nature they are climbers; budgies are hardy seed eaters and their strong beak is utilised for dehusking seeds as well as a climbing aid. When kept indoors however, it is important to supplement their diet of seeds with fresh fruit and vegetables, which would be found in the wild. Budgies are social birds, so it is most important to make sure they have company, preferably of their own kind. They do enjoy human companionship though, and may be persuaded, if gently stroked on the chest feathers to perch on one's finger. If not kept in an aviary, they need a daily period of free flight, but great care must be taken not to let them escape.

Last, but most definitely not least, perhaps the most popular breed of domestic bird, is the 'companion parrot' – a general term used for any parrot kept as a pet that interacts with its human counterpart. Generally, most species of parrot can make good companions. Common domestic parrots include large birds such as Amazons, African Greys, Cockatoos, Eclectus, Hawk-headed Parrots and Macaws; mid-sized birds such as Caiques, Conures, Quakers, Pionus, Poicephalus, Rose-Ringed parakeets and Rosellas, and many of the smaller types including Budgies, Cockatiels,

Parakeets, lovebirds, Parrotlets and Lineolated Parakeets. The Convention on International Trade in Endangered Species of Wild Fauna and Flora (also known as CITES) has made the trapping and trade of all wild parrots illegal, because taking parrots from the wild has endangered or reduced some of the rarer or more valuable species. However, many parrot species are still common; and some abundant parrot species may still be legally killed as crop pests in their native countries. Endangered parrot species are better suited to conservation breeding programs than as companions.

Parrots can be very rewarding pets to the right owners, due to their intelligence and desire to interact with people. Many parrots are very affectionate, even cuddly with trusted people, and require a lot of attention from their owners. Some species have a tendency to bond to one or two people, and dislike strangers, unless they are regularly and consistently handled by different people. Properly socialized parrots can be friendly, outgoing and confident companions. Most pet parrots take readily to trick training as well, which can help deflect their energy and correct many behavioural problems. Some owners successfully use well behaved parrots as therapy animals. In fact, many have even trained their parrots to wear parrot harnesses (most easily accomplished with young birds) so that they can be taken to enjoy themselves outdoors in a relatively safe manner without the risk of flying away.

Parrots are prey animals and even the tamest pet may fly off if spooked. Given the right care and attention, keeping birds is usually problem free. It is hoped that the reader enjoys this book.

THE BREEDING
OF COCKATIELS

The Cockatiel is a dwarf species of the Cockatoo family, originally from Australia. The Cockatiel or Cockatillo is to the Cockatoo family, what the Parrakeet is to the Parrot family.

The Cockatiel is of an ashy grey color above, with a white wing patch. The male has a bright yellow face with an orange cheek, while the cheek of the female is a much duller color, making it comparatively easy to determine the sexes. Both the male and the female have an attractive crest, which they delight in elevating.

The Cockatiel should be fed the same seeds as Parrakeets with the exception that they should also have a supply of hemp and sunflower seed. They should be fed greens, etc., the same as other birds, and should always have a liberal supply of health grit before them.

We recommend the Cockatiel highly as an aviary bird, as they are extremely hardy, are excellent breeders in captivity, are inoffensive to other cage mates, and can be associated with almost any other kind of bird in the same aviary or cage.

Being larger in size than the Parrakeet, their flying may

frighten other birds when they are first turned into the aviary, but they will soon find that the Cockatiel is harmless, and after a few days will pay no attention to him.

Their breeding is similar to Parrakeets. They do not build a nest, but instead lay their eggs in a hollow tree. Accordingly they should be furnished with a nest box of from ten to twelve inches in diametetr, with the bottom concave so the eggs will not roll apart. A small quantity of sawdust should be placed in the bottom of the nest box as this also tends to keep the eggs together.

The nest box should be at least ten inches high with an entrance hole two and one-half inches in diameter, at the front and near the top of the nest box.

Although several pairs of Cockatiels can be bred in the same aviary, much better success will be obtained by associating only one pair. They can be successfully bred in either a large cage or aviary in which there are birds of other varieties.

They lay from two to six eggs before setting and usually mature all of the young that are hatched, and will rear two or three broods each season. The hen incubates the eggs at night while the cock bird usually incubates in the daytime. The nest box can be examined occasionally during the incubation period without disturbing the birds as they are not easily frightened.

For your breeding stock select only the strongest specimens

obtainable, and be sure that they are at least two years old, as younger birds seem very restless and seldom remain on the nest for the entire incubation period. Quite often they will desert the nest before the young are hatched. If permitted to do so, they will often breed in the winter, and to prevent this the nest box should be removed in the fall, or after the third brood has been raised.

THE COCKATIEL

(*Callopsittacus novæ-hollandiæ.*)

HABITAT AND WILD LIFE.

Indigenous to Australia, breeding in the South, then migrating to the North, it is found in vast numbers. According to Gould, these birds are found breeding in the wooded flats of most of the rivers that flow to the North-West. He states he has seen the ground covered with them engaged in feeding on the seeds of mature grasses, etc., and that it was no uncommon circumstance to see them by hundreds on the dead branches of gum trees in the neighbourhood of water, which they frequently visit for the purpose of satisfying their thirst; comparing this with their similar practice in the aviary, it would appear that a constant supply of water is essential to keep them in health and condition. With the exception of the North-East corner of Queensland, they range practically over the whole of Australia. Quarrion is their native name; they are also known as the Crested Ground Parrakeet, and Grey and Yellow Top-knotted Parrot. But such names are seldom used either by dealers or aviculturists in this country.

PLUMAGE.

Adult male: The general body covering is an extremely chaste arrangement of grey and white, the contrasts of which are very striking, yet with an entire absence of harshness; this beauty of general plumage, its beautiful primrose-yellow cheeks, and its ear patches of brick-red, combine to make a really striking and handsome bird. The crest is mostly yellow, as are the cheeks; the top of head, neck, back, and wing are ashen-grey; there is a broad band of white from the shoulders over the greater wing coverts; the under parts are pale ashen-grey; tail, dark grey on its proper surface and blackish underneath; back, legs and feet, grey; iris, nut brown. Total length, 13in.; tail, 5 1/2 to 6in.

SEXUAL DISTINCTION.

The female lacks the yellow cheeks of the male; hers being grey, lightly suffused with yellow; her ear coverts are greyish-red, those of the male being bright brick-red; her crest is entirely grey, that of the male being practically all yellow; the underside of her tail is regularly barred with grey, yellow and white, that of the male being dull black.

YOUNG.

These resemble the adult hen, but are a trifle greyer, and their plumage lacks the bloom of adults. At the first moult they come into adult plumage, and cannot then be distinguished from their parents. The primrose-yellow cheeks of the males increase slightly in intensity of colour with each successive moult; this is also the case with the females, the yellow suffusion on their cheeks being much stronger on old birds than on those of, say, two years old.

They are quite blind for the first five or six days, and covered with longish yellow hairs; they soon grow, are ugly masses of pin feather at from six to fourteen days old, and are fully fledged at about three and a half weeks old (it is very difficult in a large aviary with these birds to tell their age to a day or two, as with the large amount of noise going on, the faint call of the young is almost drowned by the other aviary noises for the first few days). They leave the nest at four and a half to five weeks old, sometimes a little longer, though some writers give it as three or four weeks, but this has certainly not been my experience. They return to the nest for the first few nights, but soon settle down to roosting among the branches, and mostly in the open portion of their enclosure.

A keen observer can usually pick out the sexes even in their nest feather; in the males the front of the crest is lighter than that of the females, and the observant aviculturist will soon learn to sort out the sexes when they are about six or seven weeks old, or even earlier.

BREEDING.

In their native haunts they nest in the spouts or hollow limbs of the gum trees, so common to Australian wilds. The bird fashions some cavity to its liking, and lays its clutch of three to five white eggs (1.2 by .9 in.) on the bare wood. Incubation takes from 16 to 17 days; both sexes take part in incubation, the male during the day and the female during the night. The season is from November to February, and two broods are usually reared.

In the aviary the best nesting receptacle is either a log (obtainable from any large dealer), or a small barrel hung up longitudinally, with a 3m. diameter hole cut in one end; these birds have a mind of their own, and will use it too, and mostly choose, when in a mixed series, any receptacle but the one put up for them, as I know to my cost; I have had one season practically nullified by their annoying stupidity in this respect; they have chosen flat-bottomed boxes, and nearly all the eggs have been spoiled by rolling about. This is one of the inconveniences of keeping a variety of birds together.

They do not attempt to breed till they are two years old, and even adult birds seldom breed the first year of their occupancy of the aviary, but usually they settle down to nesting seriously the following year, and keep merrily on, only stopping (not always, for I have had young reared during this period) for the moult. They seem more prolific in the aviary than in their native wilds, sometimes as many as seven being reared as a single brood.

As the hen begins to sit with her second egg, there is fully a week between the first and last hatch when the clutch is a full one, so the young emerge at intervals, but this seldom makes any difference, for all are usually reared, and often the first out assists in feeding his brothers and sisters. It is seldom, indeed, that any mishap occurs, for with the plenitude of food to hand, and immunity from the dangers common to all wild life in their native haunts, they are practically continuous breeders in the aviary; occasionally a pair turn up that lay eggs innumerable and seldom hatch one out. With such there is nothing to do but to get rid of them (turn them loose in some park) and secure another pair.

My first brood of young were reared entirely on Canary, millet, and greenstuff, but later they had access to soft food, oats, dari, sunflower, wheat, etc., and meal worms, and they helped themselves freely to all, as also do Budgerigars. When kept in an aviary by themselves let them have a pan of Canary and white millet, and another of wheat, dari, oats, and sunflower, with green food ad lib., just what happens to be in season; they are extremely fond of grass in flower.

A liberal supply of old mortar rubbish, crushed egg-shells, and cuttlefish must be kept up, or cases of egg-binding will be frequent. I have always attended to this, and have never had a case of egg-binding with this species. If a young male is taken as soon as it can feed itself, or better, as soon as it is fully fledged, and hand-reared, it makes a charming pet as a cage bird, and learns to speak a few words. I have seen such, but have not personally so experimented with them.

GENERAL NOTES.

This is the bird par excellence for the mixed series m an outdoor aviary, for with many years' experience of these charming birds I have never known them to snap at even the smallest occupant of their enclosure. If not clad in royal purple as some of their congeners, they are certainly not plain or dull coloured birds; my oldest male (10 years at least) is a handsome fellow, the grey and white contrast of his body plumage, brilliant yellow cheeks and red ear coverts making him one of the most striking birds in the aviary, even with Red Rosellas to keep him company. When moulting he never seems to have a feather out of place, and he has never had the slightest ailment all the years he has been in any possession. It is really a shapely bird of generally fine appearance, and is of a confiding and fearless demeanour.

My birds will permit me to do anything with them. Some actually let me pick them up. They will take their food on the ground close to my feet, so long as I keep still, and on the branches will not move when I am within six inches of them, only if I attempt to lay hold of them, then they will fly to another perch near at hand, and though I have many rare and valuable birds, very few of them are more interesting. In spite of their being now comparatively common, I should certainly not care to banish them from the aviary; though I must admit I should find them trying in the house. That is their one fault; they have a voice, and they believe in using it. At the same time, I am bound to say that I have never had any of my neighbours lodge any complaints concerning them, and I can with confidence recommend the Cockatiel as an interesting and entertaining pet, especially so for the garden aviary; and as they thrive even with the roughest treatment, the veriest tyro need not hesitate to try his 'prentice hand with them. Budgerigars are not safe with Finches, etc.; but the Cockatiel I have never found to harm even the smallest Waxbill, though I have kept the species on and off for over twenty years.

THE COCKATIEL

HOW TO BREED, TAME, AND TEACH TO TALK

There can be but few fanciers who know what lovely and affectionate pets Cockatiels make when reared from the nest, or they would be much more popular than at present, for they are most easily bred and require very little attention compared with most other foreign birds. They are free breeders, will stand the coldest winter outdoors, are easily tamed, make free talkers, and will learn to whistle a tune more quickly than any bird I know.

Imported Cockatiels, like imported Budgerigars, seldom breed the first year they are in this country, being very wild, and it takes considerable time for them to settle down. Besides, their natural breeding season corresponds with our Winter. It is much the best plan to start with a good pair of aviary-bred birds; there are plenty to be got now. These would cost from £3 to £4 per pair, and would prove cheaper than half-a-dozen pairs of the cheap stuff so much advertised.

SEXING THE BIRDS.

Cockatiels are about twelve inches long, the tail accounting for about five inches. A slate grey is the predominant colour; the cock has a bright primrose-yellow face and crest, and a patch of bright red on each side, covering the ears. The hen has only a slight yellowish tinge on the face and a shade of red showing on the ears; but some hens get much brighter than others. Another distinguishing mark of the hen is the beautiful wavy lines of yellow on the under side of the tail. These lines run across, similar to the markings on a Pheasant's tail; but the outer feathers are sometimes all yellow. The young resemble the hen until the first moult. But even in the nests the young cocks have a bolder look, a fuller eye, and a more "bully" head than the hens.

One well-known writer on foreign birds has stated that Cockatiels have not the power of erecting or depressing the crest at will like the Cockatoos, but this is a mistake. If two Cockatiels show fight to each other, they will lay their crests down perfectly flat; then, if startled, the crest instantly goes up, erect as possible. Further, if you have a tame cock Cockatiel, and are fondling him, you will find the bird erects or lowers his crest according to the humour or temper he is in.

ROOM FOR BREEDING.

For breeding, an empty room with a window facing South will do very well for the purpose, but a place out of doors is greatly to be preferred. Anyone who has a small garden, or even a backyard, where there is plenty of sun, can erect in a few hours accommodation for a pair of Cockatiels. A place six feet high in front, if against a wall four or five feet long, and three or four feet from back to front, will be ample. Let it be weather-boarded on top and then tarred and thatched, or match-boarded and covered with corrugated iron. If boarded only, the sun splits the boards and so lets in the wet. Half the front may be board and half wire, and the door should be in the end where the boarding is, so that when you enter the birds will fly to the wire and not to the door through which you are entering. The door should be low, so that if the birds fly towards you when entering there will be wing space above your head.

ON BUYING BIRDS.

The next thing is to get your birds. An advertisement in "Cage Birds," stating fully your wants, will no doubt get you what you require; that is, if you do not know a breeder of these birds you can rely on. But, as I said before, don't go in for cheap birds, newly imported, or it is a hundred to one you will be disappointed. My first pair of Cockatiels I paid 30/-for, from Mr. C. W. Gedney, the popular and instructive writer on foreign birds; that was somewhere about thirty years ago. Now, £3 or £4 would be a fair price for a good pair of adult birds.

NESTING AND NEST BOXES.

Now we have our aviary up, and a pair of genuine aviary-bred birds in it, the next thing is to provide a suitable nest. Dr. Greene has recommended small barrels laid on their sides, with a hole at the end. I have tried them, but with indifferent success. I have also tried hollow branches, hollow logs, boxes with half a cocoanut husk fixed in, and also, as one writer recommends, a nesting-place made of bricks on the floor of the aviary. But none of my Cockatiels would ever look at a nest on the ground, and I have kept and bred some scores, and have several pairs breeding at the present time.

All the above nesting-places have their advantages and disadvantages, but the nest I have found the most successful, and not only for Cockatiels, but also for such birds as Rosellas, Pennants, Mealy Rosellas, etc., is made thus: Get a piece of deal 5/8in. thick and 7ins. wide (a piece of 7-in. flooring will do). Cut off three lengths 16 inches long, for two sides and top, one 22 inches long for bottom, and two 6 3/8ins. for the ends. Nail on one of the sides against the bottom, and the other side edge on to the bottom. The top will then be hinged to one side, and shut down on to the top of the other side, leaving the extra six inches of the bottom projecting for the birds to pitch upon when entering the nest. Fit in the two ends, first cutting a hole three inches in diameter near the top of the end which has the projecting piece at the bottom. One hinge to the top, if put in the centre, will be sufficient; the weight of the lid will keep it down without any fastening. This lid will be found very useful when cleaning out the nest, which cleaning will be needed before the young leave it.

If you should be fortunate and get five or six strong youngsters in one brood, as I have had many a time, they soon foul the nest, and, if allowed to get dirty, soon become sore on knees (or rather heels) and abdomen. When you have your box ready, put a layer of dry pine sawdust, about two inches deep, on the bottom of the box, pressing it well down, making a good cavity at the back for the reception of the eggs. See that there are no sharp-pointed bits of wood in the sawdust likely to prick through the shells of the eggs.

WHEN EGGS ARE LAID

After the first two or three eggs are laid it is best to look in before the hen commences to sit, to make sure that the sawdust is all right, and that the eggs are in a hollow together.

Very few hens require much attention in this respect, except wild ones, which are apt to rush out of the nest at any sudden or unusual noise, and so scatter the eggs about the box. If the cock, however, goes into the box much, the sawdust may get levelled down.

The hen lays from three to seven white eggs rather smaller than a Pigeon's. Cockatiels generally begin to sit with about the third egg; sometimes with the first, and occasionally not until the last is laid. I say Cockatiels, for the cock sits by day and the hen by night. The hen (like the Budgerigar) lays on alternate days, so that when she commences to sit with the first egg, this means, if they all hatch, a considerable difference in the age and size of the young ones. But the smallest is very seldom injured by the others; and the parents seem to look after the baby before its older brothers and sisters. I have frequently found the smallest with its crop almost bursting with food when the crops of the others seemed almost empty. Cockatiels sit about twenty days, and the young, when newly hatched, are covered with yellow, silky down.

THE USE OF BREAD.

Cockatiels are frugal feeders, and require nothing but Canary, white millet, and a few white oats. When they had young in the nest I at one time used a lot of bread for them, but I think it helps to foul the nest and keep the young very loose. Those who prefer to use bread (and some Cockatiels, if allowed, will feed their young almost entirely on it), should cut out a good piece of the crumb part of a stale loaf, and put it to soak in a bowl of cold water. After soaking ten or fifteen minutes, take it between the hands and squeeze as dry as possible, letting the water drain out between the fingers.

Cockatiels feed their young by taking their beaks inside their own (after the manner of Pigeons). Then with a pumping motion of the head the old birds bring the partly digested food from their crops into their beaks, from which the young ones feed.

COCKATOO OR PARRAKEET?

This is another characteristic, besides the moving of the crest, which, in my humble opinion, brings the Cockatiel much nearer in relationship to the Cockatoos. For among all the Parrakeets I am acquainted with (such as Rosellas, Mealy Rosellas, Ringnecks, Plumheads, Pennants, Redrumps, Budgerigars, Kings, Bloodwings), every one I can call to mind, without exception, brings the food from the crop first into the beak, and then feeds, whereas Cockatoos (at least the Rose-breasted, which I have kept in my aviaries in pairs), feed like Cockatiels, viz., take the beak of the young in their own and then pump the food from the crop. Macaws feed in the same way as Parrakeets. I have put Rosellas' eggs under Cockatiels, which hatched them all right, but although the young Rosellas stayed in the nest three days, there was never a particle of food in their crops. Whether the Cockatiels knew they were not their own progeny, or whether they could not feed them, I am unable to say. Certain it is young Cockatiels in the same nest were well fed and all reared. I think these variations in the manner of feeding the young in different birds have not had the attention they deserve from aviculturists.

HATCHING AND REARING.

But to return to our subject. Cockatiels will breed at an age of twelve months, and have three and sometimes four broods in the season. I prefer, however, a two-year-old cock, for the younger ones will sometimes take no notice whatever of the eggs, and as the hen usually leaves them in the morning (thinking she has done her share), of course the eggs get spoilt when the cock shirks his task in the daytime, preferring to sit dozing beside his wife on the roost. The latter the hen soon finds out, but how she can tell there is no life in the eggs is a mystery. Still, when such is the case, the hens scarcely ever sit their time out, but commence to lay again after about ten or fourteen days. This is very annoying, as you cannot very well tell the difference between the newly-laid ones and the spoilt ones.

The young birds leave the nest when about five weeks old, and seldom return to it again. They are able to pick up food at about six weeks, though it is hardly safe to take them away at that age, for the old ones will continue to feed them for three months, or until there is another family to attend to.

If you desire to rear some that will be very tame, it is a good plan to put them in a Parrot cage a day or two after they leave the nest, and let the old ones tend them through the wires, putting soaked seed and water in the cage as well. The cage must be wired wide enough to allow the young ones or the parent birds to easily put their heads between the wires. This method will prevent them from getting as wild as they would do if allowed to have the fly of a large aviary.

Don't forget to give some cuttlefish bone or crushed egg-shells, or both, when your birds are going to nest, otherwise you will get soft-shelled eggs and egg-bound hens, though these birds seem much freer from the latter complaint than Budgerigars. A little fresh groundsel may also be given, but do not let it stay in the aviary and get stale (or let the soaked bread go sour), or you will soon have no Cockatiels left to feed.

If fairly fortunate you will now have your young ones out of the nest and able to feed themselves, so I will devote a few remarks to taming them and teaching them to talk. Let me say at once that anyone who has a tame, talking male Cockatiel is to be envied, for such birds are the most delightful pets imaginable.

TO DISTINGUISH THE YOUNG MALES.

We will assume that we have secured our nest of young ones fully fledged and able to take care of themselves. Now we want to pick out our young cocks, either to tame and teach ourselves, or to sell for someone else to teach. This picking out of the young cocks is rather difficult, especially to a novice, for all the young resemble the mother.

I have seen the plucking of a few face feathers recommended, but this is not a bit of use. I once had nineteen young Cockatiels which left the nests at about the same time. When fully fledged, from each one I gently extracted a few feathers from the right-hand side of the face, leaving a very small bare spot. Here the plumage should have been renewed with yellow in the cock birds if this plan was a success, but the feathers came again on all of them the same colour as before. Further, strange though it may seem, when they moulted they did not shed the new feathers, and the cocks (there were twelve out of nineteen) when twelve months old, still had this little drab spot on the right-hand side of their yellow faces.

I find the best plan is to pick out the birds showing the brightest yellow tinge on the face, with the reddest earmarks, darkest and least-marked under side of tail, and with the boldest appearance about the head. If you do this, you will be pretty sure to spot the cock birds, although an experienced eye can usually pick out cocks from hens among birds which in plumage are exactly alike.

THE ART OF TAMING.

After selecting your birds, cage them separately, and the cocks will begin to warble and whistle about two or three weeks afterwards. Now is the time to commence taming operations, for they will have got used to their cages, and will be fairly quiet, providing they have not been roughly handled or frightened. Everyone who keeps birds should acquire the habit of moving gently when doing anything to or near them. Especially is this so when the taming or training of a bird is in question, for one sudden movement may undo what it has cost hours and perhaps days to accomplish. Remember, as the song says, "Gently does the trick." The following instructions will be found useful to anyone who has bought a young Cockatiel or other Parrakeet, to tame, as well as to the breeders of same. My plan, which is so successful that I have kept it a secret for many years, finding it so very remunerative, is this:—

THE FIRST LESSON.

Have the bird in a cage with the door large enough for you to put your hand in and out of it easily, and with the roost so fixed that it is easy to touch the bird's head. A square Parrot-cage is best, with the roost from side to side, so that the bird will face the door. In the evening, when the bird is asleep, turn the gas or lamp down very low, so that you can only just see the bird. Then begin talking to him gently, calling him by his name, generally "Joey," if a Cockatiel. Say "Pretty Joey," "Joey's a pretty bird," etc., in a coaxing tone, gently opening the cage door the while.

This will attract his attention, but if he be in any way frightened at this stage, when just awake, he will simply bang himself recklessly about the cage for ten minutes or so, screeching all the time, and he must be left alone for the rest of that night. Hence the necessity for being gentle.

If not frightened, your bird will now be on the watch, wondering what is going to happen. Pass your hand very slowly into the cage and above the bird's head, the palm being just above the top, so that your fingers will be in the right position to touch his poll just behind the crest. All this must be done so slowly that the bird does not notice the movement of your hand in the dark. Don't forget to repeat the above words to him while this is going on. Being unable to discern anything in the dark, his whole attention will be given to listening most intently.

KEEP ON TICKLING.

After waiting a minute, so that he will think everything is all right, with one finger, or rather with your forefinger nail, lightly touch his poll feathers. He will, no doubt, start and bob his head when first touched, but you must keep your hand perfectly still until he is again settled. Then touch him once again. He will now probably make a hissing noise, and peck forward savagely, but, finding nothing in front, is doubtless a bit puzzled. After two or three such attempts the bird will remain quiet, and let you gently tickle his poll. Here ends his first lesson.

EXPOSE YOUR HAND.

When he appears to like having his poll tickled, or scratched, get someone to turn the gas or lamp up a little higher while you are doing it, so that he can just see your hand. After he is quiet, and you are still tickling his poll, raise the light still more; then gently take your hand away, but not out of the cage. Then quietly lift your hand over his head again, moving your finger as if scratching. He may peck at you a time or two, but you need not be afraid, for Cockatiels will not hurt unless handled, and then if you do not take hold of them the right way they will very soon take hold of you; yes, and let you know it, too. When your hand is over his head, he will put his head down a little. Now is the time to tickle him again.

When this lesson is over, have the light turned full on while he is quiet and you are scratching his poll. Then draw your hand gently out of the cage. This should have occupied you about an hour. Repeat this for a night or two, and he will have lost all fear of your hand. Then, when he will allow you to put your hand into his cage with the light full on and scratch his poll without showing any fear, you may try him in the daytime, but not before. I have had birds that I could do anything with by gaslight which were very timid in the daytime, My old Toucan for twelve months would allow me to scratch his poll or stroke him by gaslight, and seemed to enjoy it, yet would not let me put my hand near him by daylight.

THE LAST STAGE.

When your Cockatiel will allow you to scratch his poll in the daytime, put your hand in the cage and go through the motions of scratching with your finger about two inches in the front of him, and he will put his head down and advance that much to have it done. You can then soon get him to put his head through the wires, or come to the cage door, or even step out on to your finger, to get his poll scratched, for with most of the Parrot and Parrakeet tribe this seems their greatest enjoyment. You now have your bird perfectly tame, and with a little coaxing he will fly from his cage and pitch on your fingers. In fact, you can now do practically as you like with him, and you have one of the most delightful pets imaginable.

SENTENCES SOON LEARNT.

A few sentences that Cockatiels learn very quickly and distinctly are "Pretty Joey," "Kiss pretty," "Joey's a beauty," "Joey wants to come out," "Let poor Joe out," "Joey wants a biscuit" (but he generally says "Kiscuit" at first). Every time you go to his cage repeat distinctly what you want him to learn. One sentence at a time, however, or he will get them all mixed up together, such as "Joey's a kiss pretty," "Kiss pretty's a beauty." When you are teaching a bird to talk, you should always speak as though you were the bird and the bird were the master or mistress. Then when he has learnt his lessons it will appear as if he is talking to you, not merely repeating what he has learnt. Many people overlook this when teaching a Parrot.

GOOD WHISTLERS SHAKE THEIR HEADS.

If you want your Cockatiel to whistle a tune (and they are good whistlers), whistle clearly and distinctly what you want them to learn. If you have two or three in separate cages, sit down and whistle a lively air to them. Watch them carefully, and you will probably see one or two of them, after listening very attentively for a minute or two, shake their heads. Pick out those that shake their heads, for they will learn to whistle a tune in half the time the others will. I had one that learned to whistle the "Sailor's Hornpipe" right through, and dance on the roost to his own whistling; and this when only nine months old. The bird was kept in a back kitchen, where I always washed my hands on coming home to meals, and I whistled the ditty while doing so. Now, in a fortnight from commencing this the bird had made a start, and as soon as I entered the house would go through the first two bars without waiting for me to begin.

PARROT OWNERS, NOTE!

I may say, in conclusion, that owners of Grey Parrots may try the same method of taming their birds, for there is no bird more fond of having its poll scratched than "Polly." If they won't allow you to do this, it is only because they are afraid of your hand and bite at you in self defence.